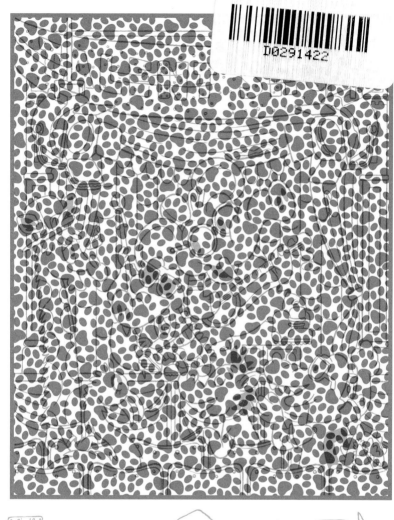

adhesive bandage

pair of pants

bacon

sandwich

sailboat

candle

spatula

slice of pizza

flashlight

sock

pliers

party hat

magnifying glass

ruler

closed umbrella

hamburger

banana

pencil

bowl

carrot

bell

1

tooth

adhesive
bandage

paddle

envelope

bell

pencil

flashlight

teacup

paper
clip

matchstick

glove

hat

saltshaker

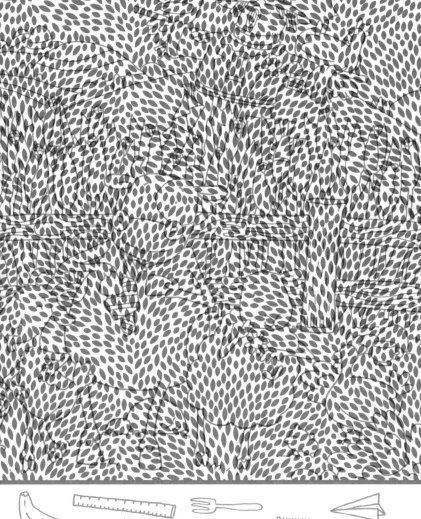

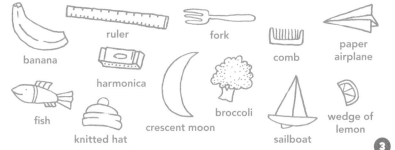

banana

ruler

fork

comb

paper airplane

harmonica

fish

broccoli

knitted hat

crescent moon

sailboat

wedge of lemon

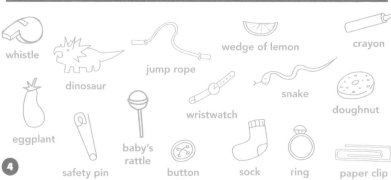

whistle

dinosaur

jump rope

wedge of lemon

crayon

eggplant

baby's rattle

wristwatch

snake

doughnut

safety pin

button

sock

ring

paper clip

teacup   toothbrush   pencil   cookie   bell   ladder

sock   magnifying glass   envelope   domino   heart

banana   kite   fried egg   slice of bread   hockey stick   2 spoons

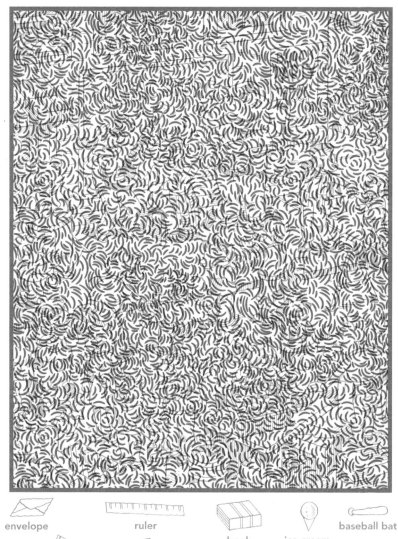

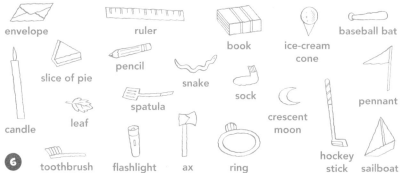

envelope

ruler

book

ice-cream cone

baseball bat

slice of pie

pencil

snake

sock

pennant

candle

leaf

spatula

crescent moon

toothbrush

flashlight

ax

ring

hockey stick

sailboat

6

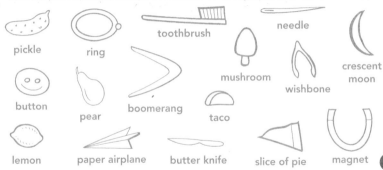

pickle

ring

toothbrush

needle

mushroom

crescent moon

wishbone

button

pear

boomerang

taco

lemon

paper airplane

butter knife

slice of pie

magnet

7

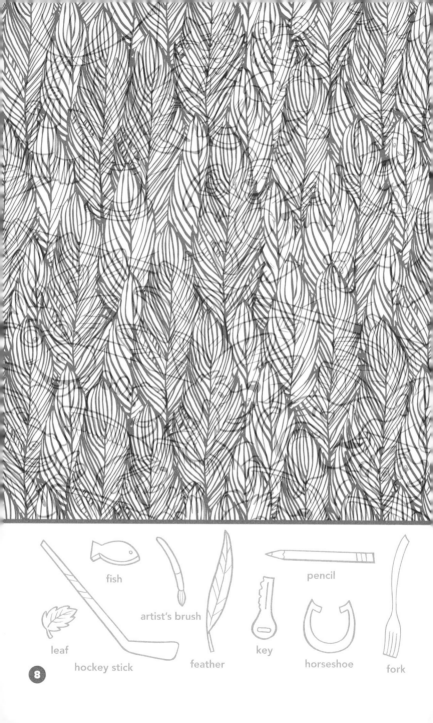

fish

artist's brush

pencil

leaf

hockey stick

feather

key

horseshoe

fork

banana

slice of pie

crown

comb

snake

ring

bowl

saltshaker

spoon

toothbrush

balloon

9

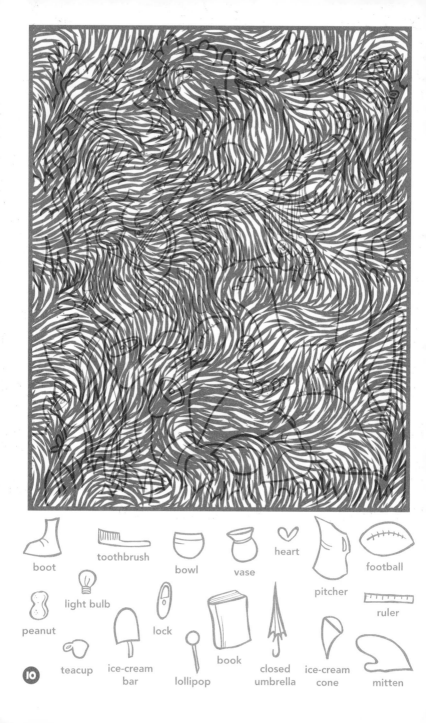

boot

toothbrush

bowl

vase

heart

pitcher

football

peanut

light bulb

lock

ruler

teacup

ice-cream bar

lollipop

book

closed umbrella

ice-cream cone

mitten

10

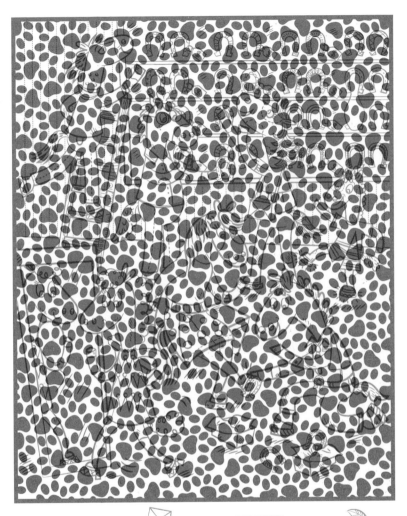

envelope

ruler

leaf

bowling pin

sailboat

slice of pizza

party hat

balloon

crown

flower

banana

mushroom

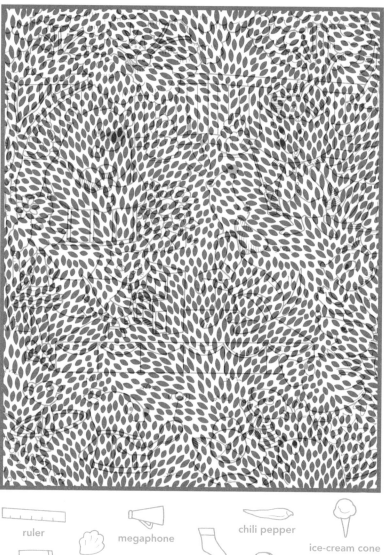

ruler

megaphone

chili pepper

ice-cream cone

seashell

sock

slice of bread

crayon

star

slice of watermelon

flag

wishbone

doughnut

crescent moon

envelope

heart

12

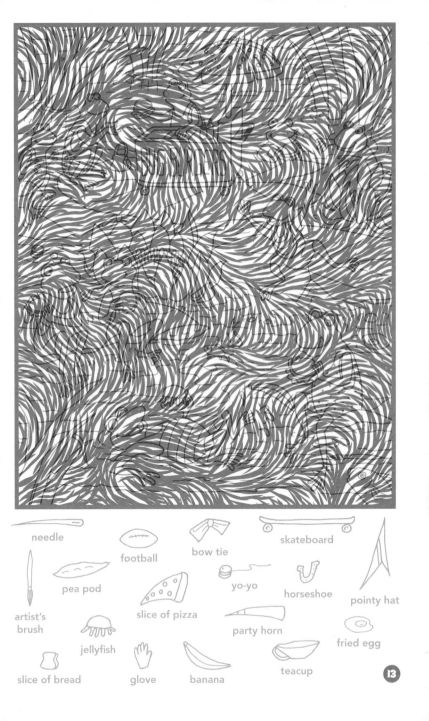

needle

football

bow tie

skateboard

pea pod

yo-yo

horseshoe

pointy hat

artist's brush

slice of pizza

party horn

fried egg

jellyfish

glove

banana

teacup

crayon

mitten

heart

mouse

banana

hockey stick

goblet

crown

boot

sailboat

horn

toothbrush

fork

slice of bread

fish

flashlight

ruler

baseball bat

fishhook

bottle

paintbrush

envelope

carrot

ladle

feather

slice of pie

lightning bolt
pennant
mitten
wedge of lemon
pickle
slice of pizza
crown
musical note
cane
spatula
toothbrush
nail
heart
pie
horseshoe

ice-cream cone

ice-cream bar

sailboat

crown

mushroom

pear

toothbrush

crayon

comb

lollipop

doughnut

baby's bottle

hammer

pennant

ruler

sock

carrot

yo-yo

pencil

skateboard

bell

spoon

broccoli

ladle

ice-cream cone

mitten

slice of pie

envelope

crescent moon

bow

hammer

drumstick

crayon

snake

strawberry

teacup

bat

paper clip

ladybug

crown

drinking straw

toothbrush

ruler

lollipop

comb

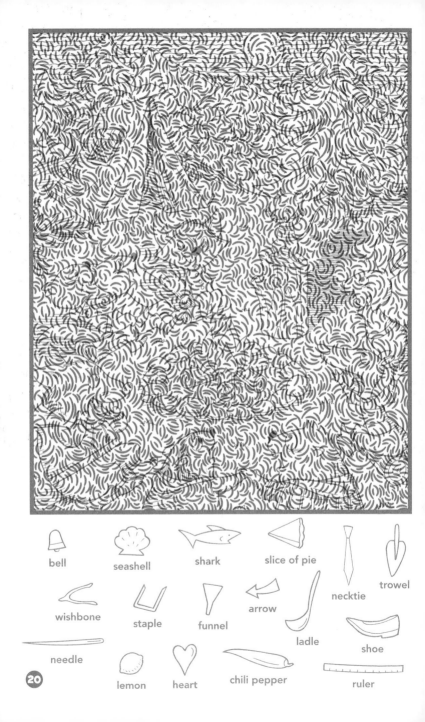

bell

seashell

shark

slice of pie

necktie

trowel

wishbone

staple

funnel

arrow

ladle

shoe

needle

lemon

heart

chili pepper

ruler

screwdriver

mitten

sailboat

ladder

dinosaur

briefcase

apple

ice-cream cone

banana

toothbrush

open book

shovel

crayon

bell

drinking straw

worm

21

domino

comb

slice of bacon

crescent
moon

ghost

glove

bowling
pin

umbrella

cotton
candy

dog bone

lollipop

adhesive
bandage

lighthouse

mitten

crown

heart

kite

shovel

rabbit

pencil

earmuffs

teacup

feather
duster

fried egg

piece of
popcorn

scissors

toy
top

mushroom

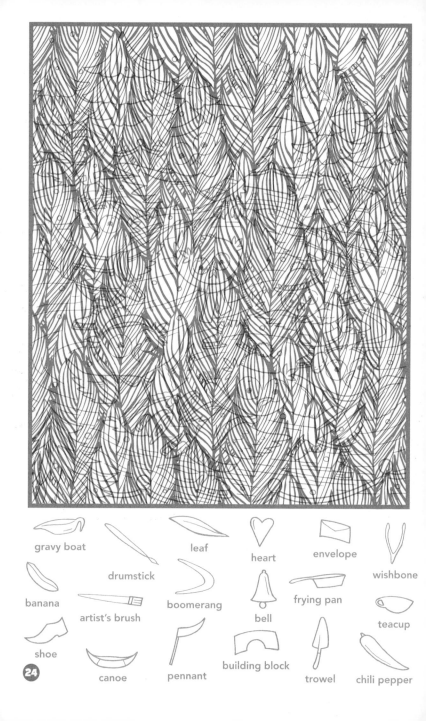

gravy boat

drumstick

leaf

heart

envelope

wishbone

banana

artist's brush

boomerang

bell

frying pan

teacup

shoe

canoe

pennant

building block

trowel

chili pepper

24

spoon wishbone needle toothbrush

ring

skillet funnel

mitten candle ax

heart crescent moon

handbag

tack lollipop

banana pennant

artist's brush

rabbit

hat

25

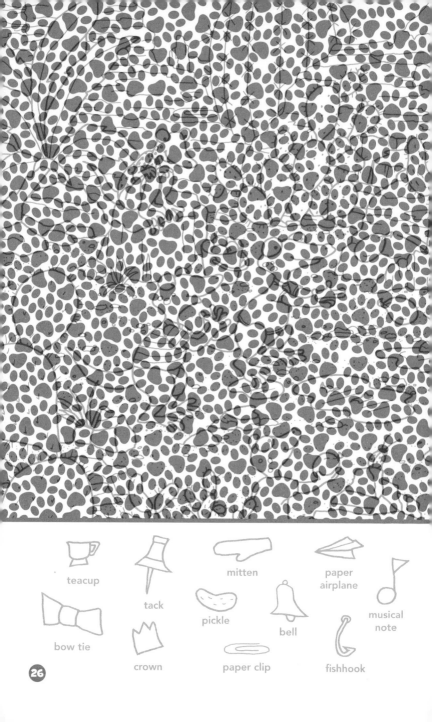

teacup

tack

mitten

paper airplane

musical note

bow tie

pickle

bell

crown

paper clip

fishhook

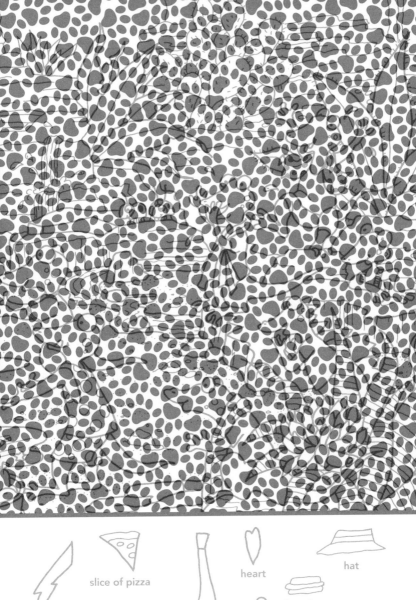

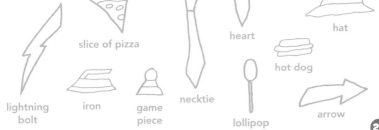

lightning bolt

slice of pizza

iron

game piece

necktie

heart

lollipop

hot dog

hat

arrow

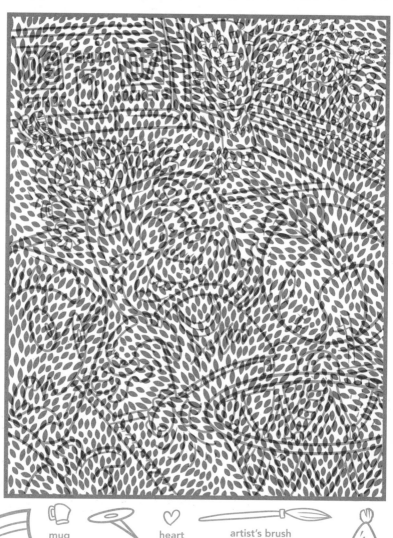

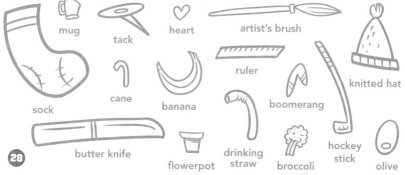

mug

tack

heart

artist's brush

ruler

knitted hat

sock

cane

banana

boomerang

butter knife

flowerpot

drinking straw

broccoli

hockey stick

olive

Page 1

Pages 2–3

Page 4

Page 5

ANSWERS

Page 6

Page 7

Pages 8–9

Page 10

Page 11

ANSWERS

Page 12

Page 13

Pages 14–15

Page 16

Page 17

ANSWERS

Pages 18–19

Page 20

Page 21

Pages 22–23